Food
ABCs

L. L. Manning

Print information available on the last page

Rev. date: 02/09/2017

To order additional copies of this book, contact:
Xlibris
1-888-795-4274
www.Xlibris.com
Orders@Xlibris.com

"In Dedication"

*To my family and friends who still believe in me as
I continue to chase my dreams, especially
my incredible siblings;
Marie, Carolyn, & Alan*

Aa is for apple, so shiny and bright

Bb is for bananas,
my favorite delight

Cc is for carrots,
so yummy and crunchy

Dd is for doughnuts,
so light and munchy

Ee is for eggplant, cooked with melted cheese

Ff is for figs,
one more, please

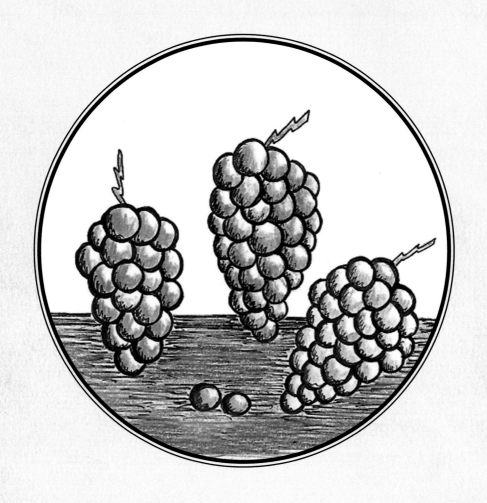

Gg is for grapes;
red, purple, and green

Hh is for honey,
so sticky and keen

Ii is for ice cream,
so creamy soft and cool

Jj is for jelly,
to eat with my "PB" at school

Kk is for kielbasa,
I love with sauerkraut

Ll is for lollipops that make me happy, without a doubt

Mm is for macaroni, with sauce or plain

Nn is for tasty nuts, that come from Spain

Oo is for oranges,
so quenching and juicy

Pp is for pizza,
so excellent and gooey

Qq is for quickbread,
like muffins and cornbread

Rr is for the rugelach,
I sneak up to bed

Ss is for spaghetti,
with sauce that I crave

Tt is for a tuna fish,
that's found in a big, blue wave

Uu is for ugly cookies, with big, silly legs

Vv is for vinegar,
when I do the Easter eggs

Ww is for watermelon,
so mouthwatering and light

Xx is for eXtra large eggs, so big and white

Yy is for yellow squash, which is okay

Zz is for zucchini,
which I'd prefer today

Printed in the United States
By Bookmasters